Delete Their Voice

Delete Their Voice

Matthew Petchinsky

1

Delete Their Voice: Become Unreachable

By: Matthew Petchinsky

DISCLAIMER

Important Notice to the Reader

Delete Their Voice: Become Unreachable is a work of personal development, emotional resilience, and self-empowerment. It is intended to support readers in reclaiming their inner autonomy, strengthening emotional boundaries, and reducing the influence of external voices that cause harm, manipulation, or self-doubt. This book is **not** a substitute for professional medical, psychological, legal, or therapeutic care.

The concepts, exercises, reflections, and frameworks presented within this book are designed for **personal growth and self-awareness only**. They are not intended to diagnose, treat, cure, or prevent any mental health condition, nor are they meant to replace professional guidance from licensed mental health providers, medical practitioners, or crisis support services.

This book does **not** encourage emotional suppression, social isolation, self-neglect, or the abandonment of healthy relationships. "Deleting their voice" refers to **reducing the internalized influence of harmful external narratives**, not cutting off communication, avoiding responsibility, or disengaging from healthy human connection. The goal is discernment, not disappearance.

If you are experiencing thoughts of self-harm, emotional overwhelm, severe depression, anxiety, trauma responses, or psychological distress, please seek immediate help from a qualified mental health professional or a trusted local crisis service. You deserve support, care, and safety.

This work also does **not** encourage manipulation, emotional withdrawal as punishment, gaslighting, or control of others. It is not a guide to dominance or avoidance. It is a guide to **inner sovereignty**, self-respect, and the cultivation of emotional boundaries that allow you to live with clarity rather than reactivity.

Any references to "silencing," "cutting off," "muting," or "becoming unreachable" are metaphorical and symbolic, referring to **internal cognitive and emotional boundaries**, not physical disappearance, abandonment of responsibilities, or disengagement from reality.

All examples, metaphors, and narratives within this book are presented for educational and reflective purposes only. Any resemblance to real persons, living or deceased, or actual events is coincidental or used symbolically.

By engaging with this book, you acknowledge that you are responsible for how you interpret and apply its insights. The author assumes no liability for actions taken based on the content of this work.

This book is an invitation—not a command—to reclaim agency, restore inner silence, and choose whose voice truly deserves access to your inner world.

Read with self-compassion.
Pause when needed.
And remember: becoming unreachable is not about disappearing—it's about becoming **unavailable to harm**.

Introduction: The People You Never Blocked Are Still in Your Head

You didn't block them.
You didn't mute them.
You didn't walk away when you should have.

And now they live in you.

Not in your phone.
Not in your inbox.
Not even in your life anymore—
but **in your mind**, where their voices still echo, comment, interrupt, judge, and narrate your every move.

This book begins with a truth most people never confront:

The loudest voices in your life are often the ones that no longer speak to you at all.

They linger as tone.
As pressure.
As hesitation.
As the pause before you act.
As the doubt that arrives just before confidence.
As the tightening in your chest when you start to feel free.

You didn't invite them to stay—but you also never removed them.

And that's not a failure.
It's a human survival response.

The Invisible Occupation

Most people believe harm only comes from active abuse, loud conflict, or ongoing contact. But the most enduring influence often comes from *former proximity*—people who once had emotional access to you and were never formally evicted.

Parents.

Partners.

Friends.

Teachers.

Bosses.

Lovers.

Authority figures.

People who once had power over your safety, approval, or belonging.

Their words didn't leave when they did.

They embedded.

You learned to hear them before you heard yourself.

You learned to pre-edit your thoughts to avoid imagined backlash.

You learned to soften your truth before it reached your mouth.

You learned to shrink your desires so they would fit inside someone else's comfort.

And eventually, you forgot where their voice ended and yours began.

That is not weakness.

That is conditioning.

Why Blocking Isn't Enough

You can block a number.
You can mute a profile.
You can delete a conversation.

But you cannot block a **pattern** without awareness.

Most people think healing means removing people from their life. But removal doesn't remove influence. The nervous system remembers. The mind repeats. The body braces.

You may have gone no-contact years ago—
yet still feel guilt when you rest.
Still hear criticism when you try something new.
Still hesitate before expressing joy, anger, or desire.

That's because **the real connection was never external**.

It was internalized.

And that is what this book is about.

The Voices That Shape You Without Permission

Some voices were loud and cruel.
Some were subtle and "well-meaning."
Some wore the mask of love, concern, or advice.

But all of them had one thing in common:
They taught you to distrust your own inner signal.

Maybe it sounded like:

- "You're too much."
- "You're not ready."
- "Be realistic."
- "Who do you think you are?"
- "You'll fail."
- "Don't embarrass yourself."
- "You should be grateful."
- "You're overreacting."
- "That's not how the world works."

Over time, these phrases stop sounding like *them* and start sounding like *truth*.

That's how control survives without contact.

This Is Not About Becoming Cold or Isolated

Let's be clear:

This book is not about emotional shutdown, detachment, or disappearing from life.

You are not here to become numb.

You are here to become **selective**.

There is a difference between being unreachable and being unreachable **to harm**.

Becoming unreachable means:

- You no longer outsource your self-worth.
- You stop negotiating with internalized critics.
- You recognize which voices deserve access to your inner world—and which do not.

It is not silence.

It is discernment.

Why "Delete" Is a Metaphor, Not an Escape

You cannot erase the past.
You cannot unhear what was said.
But you can **change the authority** those voices have over your present.

Deleting a voice does not mean pretending it never existed.
It means revoking its power to define you.

It means recognizing:

- Some voices were never meant to be permanent.
- Some opinions were formed from someone else's fear.
- Some expectations were never yours to carry.

This book is not about becoming hardened.
It's about becoming **unavailable to distortion**.

Becoming Unreachable Is an Act of Self-Respect

When you stop responding to internalized noise, something strange happens:

- Your decisions become quieter—but clearer.
- Your confidence feels less performative and more grounded.
- You stop explaining yourself to people who were never listening.
- You stop asking for permission to exist as you are.

Unreachability is not distance.
It is clarity without apology.
And it is learned.

What This Book Will Help You Do

Over the pages ahead, you will learn how to:

- Identify which voices in your mind are not yours
- Recognize how emotional conditioning shaped your self-talk
- Detach from internalized authority without guilt or rebellion
- Reclaim your internal narrative without aggression or avoidance
- Build an inner environment that feels safe, quiet, and sovereign

This is not about fixing yourself.
It's about remembering who you were before you were edited.

A Final Truth Before We Begin

You don't owe access to anyone who taught you to doubt yourself.

You don't owe loyalty to voices that grew from fear, control, or projection.

And you don't need permission to protect your inner world.

Some people were meant to be chapters.
Not narrators.

And some voices were never meant to be heard again.

Welcome to the work of becoming unreachable.

Chapter 1: Echoes in the Skull

The First Voice You Learned to Trust

The first voice you ever trusted was not your own.

Before language was yours, before thought felt personal, your nervous system learned safety by tuning itself to others. Tone came before meaning. Volume before intention. Approval before identity. You learned whether you were safe by the sound of someone else's breath, the pause in their response, the way silence stretched when you spoke too freely.

This is not weakness. This is biology. The human brain is wired to survive through attunement. We listen before we understand. We mirror before we decide. And in those early moments, the voices around you became more than sound—they became *signals*. Signals of safety. Signals of danger. Signals of love withheld or granted.

Those early signals etched grooves into your inner world. Over time, they stopped sounding external. They became internal narrators. A tone of disappointment that appears when you rest. A warning when you feel joy. A tightening when you consider wanting more. You may not recognize the voice, but you feel its authority.

This is how echoes begin—not as trauma, but as adaptation.

And adaptations, once useful, can outlive their purpose.

The first voice you trusted may no longer be present in your life, but its echo still shapes how you interpret the world. It whispers not in words, but in sensation—hesitation, guilt, second-guessing. You don't hear it; you *obey* it.

The Architecture of Internal Noise

Your mind is not loud by accident. It is crowded because it learned that survival required constant monitoring. Every raised eyebrow, every unpredictable mood, every emotional shift trained your awareness to scan and anticipate.

This is how noise is built: repetition plus emotion equals imprint.

When something happens often enough during moments of vulnerability, it hardens into internal law. A sigh becomes a verdict. A look becomes a threat. A raised voice becomes a rule. And your nervous system, brilliant and terrified, stores it all for later use.

Eventually, you stop reacting to people—you react to *memory*.

You replay conversations that never finished. You rehearse responses for arguments that may never come. You explain yourself to no one. You defend yourself in rooms where you're completely alone.

That is the echo chamber of the mind.

It doesn't shout. It hums. It simulates danger long after the threat has passed, because once, long ago, that vigilance kept you safe.

But what protected you then may now be the very thing keeping you trapped.

When Echoes Become Identity

There is a moment—quiet and devastating—when you realize the voice judging you sounds familiar not because it is yours, but because you were trained to carry it.

This is where identity begins to blur.

You think you are cautious, but you are actually afraid.

You think you are humble, but you are suppressing yourself.

You think you are disciplined, but you are scared of punishment that no longer exists.

The echo becomes a substitute for authority. You don't need anyone else to limit you; you do it automatically. You correct yourself before anyone can. You shrink before anyone asks. You apologize for taking up space that was always yours.

And slowly, you forget that your inner world was ever meant to be yours alone.

The danger is not the memory—it's the loyalty.

When we remain loyal to internalized voices that harmed us, we confuse familiarity with truth. We confuse survival with identity. We mistake endurance for wisdom.

The echo survives because you believe it keeps you safe. But safety that requires silence is not safety—it is containment.

The Body Remembers What the Mind Denies

Even when you tell yourself you're "fine," your body often disagrees.

Your shoulders tighten before your mind understands why. Your breath shortens when you're about to speak honestly. Your chest contracts when you consider choosing yourself.

This is because the body keeps records the mind edits.

The echo doesn't live only in thought—it lives in posture, in breath, in muscle memory. It's the flinch before feedback, the exhaustion after setting a boundary, the shame that appears without invitation.

You may try to reason with it, but the body doesn't respond to logic. It responds to safety. And for many, safety was once conditional.

So the body learned: *Stay small. Stay quiet. Stay acceptable.*

This is not weakness. It is intelligence shaped by necessity.

But what once protected you may now be preventing you from inhabiting your full self. The body is still waiting for proof that the danger has passed.

Hearing the Echo Without Obeying It

The goal is not to destroy the echo.

The goal is to recognize it without submission.

When you notice the voice—when it tightens your chest or stalls your decision—you can pause. You can ask: *Whose voice is this? When did I learn it? What was it trying to protect me from?*

This question alone begins to loosen its grip.

You are not required to argue with the echo. You are not required to silence it violently. You are only asked to stop mistaking it for truth.

There is power in observation without reaction. When you witness the echo rather than merge with it, space appears. In that space, choice becomes possible.

And choice is the beginning of freedom.

You don't need to erase your past to move forward. You only need to stop letting it narrate your present.

The Moment You Become the Listener Instead

At some point, something shifts. You notice the echo arise—and you remain still. You don't flinch. You don't obey. You don't argue.

You listen, and then you choose differently.

This is the moment the internal hierarchy changes.

The voice that once ruled becomes just another sound in the room. It no longer decides your worth. It no longer predicts your future. It becomes data, not destiny.

You begin to hear *your* voice underneath it—quieter at first, uncertain, but unmistakably yours.

That voice doesn't rush.

It doesn't shame.

It doesn't threaten.

It simply tells the truth.

And the truth sounds like relief.

Journal Prompts

1. What is the most familiar critical voice in my head, and when did I first hear it?
2. What does this voice try to protect me from?
3. How does my body react when this voice appears?
4. In what moments do I silence myself without being asked?
5. What belief about myself did I learn from this voice?
6. When have I mistaken fear for intuition?
7. What would change if I questioned this voice instead of obeying it?
8. Whose approval am I still unconsciously seeking?
9. What part of me feels safest when I am quiet?
10. What might my own voice sound like if I gave it room to speak?

Closing Reflection

The echoes in your skull are not enemies. They are remnants of survival—old maps drawn in dangerous terrain. But you are no longer where you once were.

You are allowed to update your inner landscape.

You are allowed to question the voices that shaped you without blaming yourself for learning their language. You are allowed to choose a quieter, kinder authority within.

This chapter is not about silencing the past.

It is about recognizing that you are no longer living inside it.

The echo may remain—but it no longer leads.

You do.

Chapter 2: Auditory Parasites

When Thoughts Are Not Yours

Not every thought you hear belongs to you.
Some arrive uninvited, already formed, already heavy, already carrying judgment you didn't choose. These are not spontaneous creations of your mind—they are **inherited intrusions**, fragments of other people's unresolved fears, expectations, and control mechanisms that have taken up residence in your inner world.

An auditory parasite is not simply a negative thought. It is a *foreign pattern* that feeds on your attention. It repeats because repetition keeps it alive. It mimics your voice so convincingly that you mistake it for intuition or realism. And because it sounds familiar, you rarely question its origin.

These parasites often enter during moments of vulnerability—childhood dependence, emotional exposure, exhaustion, trauma, or love mixed with fear. They attach themselves to survival instincts and disguise themselves as guidance.

They don't shout. They whisper.

They sound reasonable. They sound like "just being realistic." They sound like protection. And that is why they persist.

The goal of this chapter is not to fight these voices—but to **identify them as foreign bodies** so they stop feeding on your attention.

How Auditory Parasites Take Root

Auditory parasites embed through repetition and authority. When someone's words carry emotional weight—fear, anger, approval, withdrawal—they bypass logic and lodge directly into the nervous system.

Your brain doesn't store them as opinions; it stores them as *rules*.

Once embedded, these voices activate automatically under stress. They surface when you are tired, hopeful, exposed, or close to choosing something meaningful. They do not ask permission. They simply begin narrating.

Over time, the line between your authentic thought and the parasite blurs. You begin to believe that your inner resistance is wisdom, that your self-doubt is maturity, that your shrinking is humility.

This is how a parasite survives: it convinces you it is protecting you.

But protection that limits growth is not protection—it is containment disguised as care.

The Seven Auditory Parasites

Below are seven common auditory parasites. Each one thrives on repetition and weakens when recognized.

1. The Doubter

Voice: "You're not ready yet."

Function: Delays action indefinitely.

Removal: Act before certainty arrives. Readiness is a byproduct, not a prerequisite.

2. The Minimizer

Voice: "It's not that serious."

Function: Shrinks your pain so it never gets addressed.

Removal: Name the impact instead of the event. Pain does not require permission.

3. The Perfectionist

Voice: "If it's not flawless, don't begin."

Function: Prevents expression through impossible standards.

Removal: Release work before it feels finished. Completion dissolves control.

4. The Guilt-Engine

Voice: "You're selfish for wanting more."

Function: Keeps you loyal to depletion.

Removal: Redefine self-respect as responsibility, not betrayal.

5. The Catastrophizer

Voice: "If you try, everything will collapse."

Function: Freezes growth through imagined disaster.

Removal: Ground in evidence, not imagination.

6. The Echo of Authority

Voice: "They know better than you."

Function: Transfers your power outward.

Removal: Ask whose life they were speaking from—not yours.

7. The Inner Jailor

Voice: "Stay small. Stay safe. Don't be seen."

Function: Maintains survival through invisibility.

Removal: Practice visibility in small, controlled ways.

These are not enemies. They are outdated guardians. But guardians who refuse to evolve become jailers.

Why the Parasites Feel Like You

Auditory parasites borrow your tone, your vocabulary, your emotional cadence. They feel intimate because they were installed during moments of intimacy—fear, love, dependency, confusion.

The brain prefers familiarity over freedom. Even harmful patterns feel safer than uncertainty. That is why these voices feel convincing. They wear your skin.

But familiarity is not truth.

The moment you notice a thought feels *automatic*, *repetitive*, or *emotionally charged without context*, you are likely hearing an echo—not insight.

Awareness doesn't kill the parasite immediately. It starves it. Attention is its oxygen. Curiosity without obedience is the beginning of detox.

You do not need to fight your mind. You only need to stop feeding what harms you.

Interrupting the Loop

Interruption is not force. It is redirection.

When a parasitic thought appears, do not argue. Instead, name it. Labeling creates distance. Distance creates choice.

You might say:

"This is the Doubter speaking."

"This is the Guilt-Engine again."

"This is not my voice."

Then return to the body. Breathe. Ground. Move. The body interrupts what the mind loops.

Over time, the parasite weakens because it no longer receives unconscious belief. It still appears—but quieter, thinner, less convincing.

You are not erasing thought. You are reclaiming authorship.

Reclaiming the Inner Channel

Your mind is not meant to be a crowded room. It is meant to be a signal space—clear, responsive, alive.

As you learn to recognize auditory parasites, something subtle happens: silence begins to feel safe. Not empty. Spacious.

In that space, your authentic voice emerges—not loud, not aggressive, but steady.

This voice doesn't demand. It invites.
It doesn't shame. It clarifies.
It doesn't rush. It waits.

This is the voice you are learning to hear again.

And once you hear it, the others lose their power.

Journal Prompts

1. Which of the seven auditory parasites do I hear most often?
2. When did I first learn to listen to this voice?
3. What does this voice claim to protect me from?
4. How has it limited my growth?
5. What happens in my body when it speaks?
6. What would happen if I didn't obey it for one day?
7. Which voices in my life taught me this pattern?
8. How does my authentic voice feel different?
9. What would safety look like without this parasite?
10. What would I say if I trusted myself completely?

Closing Reflection

You were never broken for hearing these voices.
You were adaptive. You were learning how to survive.

But survival is not the same as living.

Auditory parasites lose power the moment you recognize them as visitors, not rulers. You do not need to evict them violently. You only need to stop feeding them your attention.

Your mind is not a battlefield.
It is a sanctuary learning to close its doors.

And the more you listen inward with discernment, the quieter the echoes become—until what remains is not noise, but knowing.

Chapter 3: Rewiring Inner Sound

The Architecture of Inner Sound

Before words, there was vibration.
Before meaning, there was tone.
Before thought, there was rhythm.

Your inner world is not built from sentences—it is built from **sound patterns**. Even when no words are present, something is always humming beneath awareness. A tension. A pulse. A cadence that tells your body whether it is safe or threatened, open or guarded.

This is your inner soundscape.

Most people believe thoughts create emotions, but the truth runs deeper: **sound creates thought**. The internal tone you carry—sharp, rushed, tense, heavy, calm—determines how thoughts form and how long they stay. A harsh internal frequency creates harsh interpretations. A steady one creates space.

This is why some people can experience the same event and walk away unshaken while others spiral. Their inner soundscape filters reality before logic ever engages.

Rewiring inner sound is not about positive thinking. It is about **retuning the internal environment** so the mind no longer defaults to threat.

The Damage of Unconscious Frequencies

When you grow up around instability, criticism, or emotional unpredictability, your nervous system learns to tune itself to chaos. Not because chaos feels good—but because it feels *familiar*.

Over time, your inner sound becomes sharp, fast, or oppressive. Even silence becomes loud. Stillness feels unsafe. Peace feels suspicious.

This is why rest can feel uncomfortable. Why joy feels temporary. Why calm can trigger anxiety.

Your inner sound has been trained to expect disruption.

And once that frequency is set, the mind begins to generate thoughts that match it. You don't think anxious thoughts because you're anxious; you feel anxious because your inner tone is already vibrating at that pitch.

To change the thoughts, you must first change the sound.

The Difference Between Silence and Stillness

Many people believe healing means silencing the mind. This creates resistance. Silence can feel like suffocation when you're used to noise.

Stillness, however, is different.

Stillness is *presence without pressure*.

It is the moment when the inner sound softens just enough for you to notice it without drowning in it. Stillness allows choice. Silence demands control.

Your goal is not to mute yourself. It is to retune.

When inner sound softens, your thoughts reorganize naturally. The urgency dissolves. The static thins. What remains is not emptiness—but clarity.

This is the foundation of rewiring.

The Rewiring Ritual: Reclaiming Inner Sound

This ritual is not mystical, though it may feel profound. It is a nervous-system recalibration designed to replace reactive noise with conscious presence.

Do not rush it. This is not a performance. It is a conversation with your inner acoustics.

Step 1: Locate the Noise

Sit or lie in a comfortable position. Close your eyes if it feels safe.

Bring attention to your inner soundscape—not your thoughts, but the *tone beneath them*.

Ask gently:

- Is it tight or loose?
- Fast or slow?
- Heavy or light?
- Sharp or dull?

Do not judge. Simply observe.

Now notice where it lives in your body. Chest? Throat? Jaw? Gut?

Place a hand there.

You are not trying to change it yet. You are letting it know it has been heard.

This step teaches your system that awareness does not equal danger.

Step 2: Introduce a New Frequency

Once you can sense the existing tone, introduce a contrasting one—softly.

This can be done through:

- A slow exhale through the mouth
- A hum
- A low, steady breath sound
- A whispered vowel (like "ah" or "oh")

Choose one and repeat it gently.

Do not overpower the existing sound. Let the new tone sit beside it.

Imagine you are tuning an instrument, not forcing it into silence.

As you do this, notice what changes. The body often responds before the mind. Muscles soften. Breath deepens. The internal pressure shifts.

You are teaching your system a new reference point.

Step 3: Anchor the New Pattern

Now introduce intention.

Quietly say (internally or aloud):

"This is the sound of safety."

"This is the sound I return to."

"This is mine."

Stay with this for 1–3 minutes. Not longer. You are building trust, not endurance.

When thoughts arise, let them float past like radio static. You are tuning into a different channel now.

End by placing a hand over your chest or abdomen and noticing the after-effect. That sensation—however subtle—is the new baseline.

Repeat this ritual daily, especially after emotional activation. Over time, the body will begin to default to this frequency instead of the old one.

When the Old Noise Tries to Return

It will.

Rewiring is not erasure. It is replacement through repetition.

Old patterns surface when you are tired, stressed, or emotionally exposed. This does not mean failure. It means your system is reaching for what it knows.

When this happens, do not fight it.

Say internally:

"I know this sound. And I know another one too."

Then return to the ritual—not to fix yourself, but to remind your system of choice.

Each time you do this, the new pathway strengthens. The old one weakens. Not because you fight it—but because you stop feeding it.

Living From the Rewired Frequency

Over time, you may notice subtle changes:

- Decisions feel less frantic.
- Your inner dialogue softens.
- Silence feels supportive instead of threatening.
- You respond rather than react.

This is not numbness. This is alignment.

Your inner sound becomes a place of rest instead of resistance. You begin to trust yourself—not because you're certain, but because you're steady.

This is the work beneath all other work.

Journal Prompts

1. What does my inner sound feel like right now?
2. When did I first learn this tone?
3. How does my body respond when I soften my breath?
4. What sound feels most regulating to me?
5. Where do I feel tension when I try to be still?
6. What changes when I allow quiet instead of forcing silence?
7. What emotion appears when the noise fades?
8. What does safety sound like in my body?
9. How can I practice this ritual daily without pressure?
10. What part of me is beginning to trust again?

Closing Reflection

Rewiring inner sound is not about becoming peaceful all the time. It is about becoming *familiar* with peace when it arrives.

Your inner world does not need to be conquered. It needs to be heard, then gently retuned.

Every time you choose presence over panic, you rewrite your internal language.

And eventually, the sound that once overwhelmed you becomes the rhythm that carries you forward.

You are not silencing yourself.

You are finally learning how to listen.

Chapter 4: Voice Erasure Rituals

The Difference Between Suppression and Erasure

Most people try to silence inner noise through force. They distract themselves, drown it out, argue with it, or pretend it isn't there. That is suppression—and suppression always fails eventually.

Erasure is different.

Erasure is not about fighting a voice. It is about **withdrawing belief from it**. A voice without belief loses its grip. A thought without authority dissolves on its own.

Suppression tightens the knot.
Erasure loosens the source.

To erase a voice is not to deny its existence, but to revoke its role. It is the conscious act of saying: *You may speak, but you no longer decide.*

This chapter is about ceremonial disengagement. About consciously stepping out of internal contracts you never agreed to sign. About ending agreements that were formed in fear, dependency, or confusion.

Voice erasure is not violence.
It is sovereignty.

Why Ritual Works When Logic Fails

Ritual bypasses the analytical mind and speaks directly to the nervous system.

Your inner world learned through repetition, tone, symbolism, and emotional imprint—not through logic alone. That is why explaining things to yourself rarely changes how you *feel*.

Ritual speaks the same language your conditioning was written in.

When done with intention, ritual creates a moment where your nervous system recognizes transition. It marks a boundary between "before" and "after." It tells the subconscious: *something has ended.*

Ritual is not superstition.

It is structured meaning.

And meaning reorganizes perception.

The rituals in this chapter are not spiritual obligations or belief systems. They are psychological rewiring practices designed to help your system release voices that no longer belong.

Ritual One: The Severing of Borrowed Voices

Purpose:

To consciously detach from internalized voices that originated outside of you and reclaim your internal authority.

Preparation

Choose a quiet space where you will not be interrupted for at least 15 minutes. You may sit or stand. Lighting is optional but softer environments often help the body relax.

You will need:

- A piece of paper
- A pen
- A small object to represent weight (a stone, key, coin, etc.)

Step 1: Naming the Voice

On the paper, write the phrase:

"This is the voice of __________."

Fill in the blank with a description, not a name if that feels safer. Examples:

- "Disappointment"
- "Control"
- "Fear of being seen"
- "Never enough"

Do not overthink it. Write what feels charged.

Now read it aloud once.

Notice what happens in your body.

Step 2: Acknowledgment Without Submission

Place your hand over your chest and say:

"You were formed to protect me.
You no longer get to lead me."

Let the words land. Do not rush past discomfort. The goal is not to banish, but to acknowledge without obedience.

Then say:

"I release the role you were never meant to hold."

As you say this, place the weight object in your hand. Feel its gravity. This represents the burden you've been carrying.

Step 3: Physical Release

Stand up. Hold the object firml

Say aloud:

"I return this weight to the past."

Then place the object on the ground, a table, or away from your body.

You are not throwing it away—you are placing it outside of yourself.

Take one full breath and notice the difference in your posture.

This is not symbolic imagination. This is embodied separation.

Step 4: Closure

Fold the paper and place it somewhere out of sight. You are not destroying it—you are removing its dominance.

Say quietly:

"This voice no longer speaks for me."

Sit in stillness for one full minute.

The ritual is complete.

Ritual Two: The Reclaiming of the Inner Channel

Purpose:

To establish a new internal authority that replaces the erased voice with presence, choice, and self-trust.

This ritual builds rather than removes.

Step 1: Grounding the Body

Sit comfortably with both feet touching the ground.

Place one hand on your chest and one on your lower abdomen.

Take three slow breaths, counting to four on the inhale and six on the exhale.

With each exhale, imagine your weight settling downward.

This signals safety.

Step 2: Establish the Signal

Now choose a physical signal that will represent your internal authority. This could be:

- Pressing thumb and finger together
- Placing a hand over your heart
- Sitting up straighter

This signal will become your "return point."

Perform the gesture now and say internally:

"This is my voice."

Let the words be simple. No force. No performance.

Step 3: Install the New Tone

Bring attention to your inner sound. Instead of changing it, *invite* a new quality—steady, calm, neutral.

Imagine a tone like a low hum or a slow wave.

Say internally:

"I choose clarity over noise."

"I choose presence over reaction."

Repeat once.

Let your body absorb the statement rather than analyze it.

Step 4: Seal the Channel

Take one final breath and say:

"This channel is mine to keep."

Hold your chosen gesture for five seconds.

Then release.

The ritual is complete.

Integration: When Old Voices Return

They will return.

Not because the ritual failed—but because the nervous system tests change before accepting it.

When an old voice resurfaces, do not panic. Recognize it as a memory echo, not a command.

Use your gesture. Use your breath. Recall the feeling of release.

The power is not in repetition alone—it is in recognition.

Each time you respond differently, the old pattern weakens.

Living Without Internal Interference

When voices lose their authority, something unexpected happens: you begin to hear yourself.

Not loudly. Not dramatically.

But clearly.

Your decisions feel grounded. Your reactions soften. Your sense of self becomes less negotiable.

You stop needing permission to exist the way you do.

That is the quiet power of erasure.

Journal Prompts

1. Which voice felt most difficult to release, and why?
2. What did my body feel during the first ritual?
3. What surprised me about the experience?
4. When have I mistaken obedience for safety?
5. How does my inner world feel after the ritual?
6. What does my true inner voice sound like?
7. When do old voices try to return?
8. What helps me feel grounded when they do?
9. What does authority feel like in my body?
10. What would change if I trusted myself fully?

Closing Reflection

Voice erasure is not destruction.
It is discernment.

You are not losing parts of yourself—you are reclaiming authorship.

What remains after the noise fades is not emptiness.
It is presence.

And presence is the beginning of freedom.

You are no longer governed by echoes.

You are speaking from within.

Chapter 5: Pure Signal Living

When the Noise Finally Falls Away

There is a moment—quiet, almost unremarkable—when you realize something is missing.

Not something you lost, but something that stopped intruding.

The constant internal commentary has softened.

The urgency has loosened its grip.

The need to explain yourself has gone quiet.

This is not emptiness.

It is *clarity*.

Pure signal living begins when the background static fades enough for you to hear what was always underneath. It does not arrive with fireworks or revelation. It arrives gently, like realizing you've been breathing shallowly and suddenly remembering how to exhale.

This state is not perfection. It is presence without distortion.

You are no longer reacting to imagined threats, inherited judgments, or internalized demands. You are responding to *what is actually happening now*. That is the essence of pure signal.

The Difference Between Noise and Signal

Noise demands attention.

Signal invites alignment.

Noise is urgent, repetitive, and emotionally charged. It speaks in extremes—*always, never, must, should*. It interrupts, rushes, and pressures.

Signal is calm. It does not beg. It does not shout. It arrives with steadiness and clarity, often without emotion attached. It feels obvious once you notice it.

Noise drains you.

Signal grounds you.

Noise fragments focus.

Signal organizes energy.

When you live from noise, your life feels reactive. You move because something pushes you. When you live from signal, your movement comes from coherence. You act because something *aligns*.

This is not about becoming passive. It is about becoming precise.

Recognizing the Texture of True Signal

Pure signal has a texture to it. It feels different in the body than anxiety or impulse.

It often arrives as:

- A quiet certainty rather than excitement
- A calm "yes" without justification
- A grounded "no" without guilt
- A sense of right timing rather than urgency

Signal does not demand immediate action. It allows choice.

You may notice that when you follow true signal, the body softens rather than tenses. Breath deepens. The jaw loosens. Thoughts simplify.

This is because true signal originates from coherence between mind, body, and values—not from fear or external pressure.

Signal does not argue with you. It waits.

Living Without Internal Interference

When internal interference fades, something profound happens: you stop negotiating with yourself.

Decisions no longer require excessive mental debate. You feel less pulled between options and more oriented toward alignment.

This does not mean life becomes effortless. It means resistance becomes informative instead of paralyzing.

You begin to trust your internal pacing. You rest when rest is needed. You move when movement is right. You speak when something is true, not when something is loud.

Living in pure signal means you no longer confuse intensity with importance. You stop chasing emotional spikes and start honoring internal consistency.

Your life becomes quieter—but more intentional.

The Discipline of Staying Tuned

Pure signal living is not a permanent state achieved once. It is a practice of listening and recalibrating.

Noise will return. Old patterns will attempt to reassert themselves. External chaos will still exist. But now, you have a reference point.

You can ask:

- Is this noise or signal?
- Is this urgency or alignment?
- Is this fear or clarity?

These questions are not judgments. They are tuning tools.

Each time you choose to listen inward rather than react outward, you strengthen your internal signal. Over time, it becomes the default.

This is not isolation. It is sovereignty.

Living as a Clear Channel

When you live from pure signal, your presence changes. People feel it even if they can't name it.

You speak less but mean more.
You react less but act with precision.
You stop proving and start embodying.

This is not detachment—it is integration.

Your inner world and outer actions begin to match. The gap between intention and behavior narrows. Life feels simpler not because it is easy, but because it is honest.

You become someone who listens deeply—to yourself, to others, to the moment.

And in that listening, you finally hear your own voice clearly.

Journal Prompts

1. How does my body feel when I am in alignment?
2. What sensations tell me I am in noise rather than signal?
3. When have I mistaken urgency for importance?
4. What does clarity feel like in my body?
5. How do I know when a choice is coming from fear?
6. What helps me return to presence quickly?
7. Where in my life am I still reacting instead of responding?
8. What does my internal "yes" feel like?
9. What happens when I slow down enough to listen?
10. What would change if I trusted my signal completely?

Closing Reflection

Pure signal living is not about perfection.

It is about alignment.

It is the quiet confidence of knowing when to move and when to wait.

The peace of no longer arguing with yourself.

The strength of acting from clarity instead of fear.

When you live from signal, your life becomes less reactive and more intentional. You stop chasing validation and start honoring resonance.

The world may still be loud—but you are no longer tuned to its chaos.

You are tuned to yourself.

And that is where true freedom begins.

Appendix A: Audio Detox Blueprint

The *Audio Detox Blueprint* is not about silence, deprivation, or removing sound from your life. It is about **reclaiming authorship over what enters your nervous system**. Sound is one of the most powerful regulators of emotion, identity, memory, and belief. Long before logic forms, sound conditions safety, fear, belonging, and urgency.

This blueprint is designed to help you **reset your auditory environment**, reduce subconscious interference, and rebuild a relationship with sound that supports clarity, sovereignty, and self-trust.

This is not a detox of sound itself.

It is a detox of **unconscious influence**.

Understanding Audio Saturation

Modern life is saturated with sound that was never designed for nervous system health:

- Constant background noise
- Algorithm-driven audio designed to provoke reaction
- Music engineered for emotional manipulation
- Voices that compete for attention rather than offer presence

When the nervous system is constantly stimulated, it loses its ability to distinguish signal from noise. Everything begins to feel urgent. Rest feels unsafe. Silence feels wrong.

This is not a personal failure—it is environmental conditioning.

The purpose of an audio detox is to **restore your capacity to choose what enters you**, rather than absorbing whatever is loudest or most frequent.

The Three Phases of Audio Detox

Phase 1: Reduction (Creating Space)

This phase is about *lessening volume*, not eliminating sound.

Practices:

- Reduce passive audio (TV running, background videos, constant podcasts).
- Choose silence during routine tasks: showering, walking, cooking.
- Lower volume levels intentionally—even music should sit beneath awareness.

What Happens:

At first, discomfort may arise. Restlessness. Boredom. Emotional surfacing.

This is normal. You are encountering the unfiltered signal beneath constant stimulation.

Do not rush to fill the space.

Silence is not emptiness—it is a calibration field.

Phase 2: Discernment (Choosing Sound with Intention)

Once the nervous system recalibrates, reintroduce sound with purpose.

Ask before pressing play:

- *Why am I choosing this sound?*
- *What state does it create in me?*
- *Does it support or scatter my attention?*

Begin to notice patterns:

- Some voices soothe but drain.
- Some energize but agitate.
- Some calm but numb.

This is not about judgment. It is about data.

You are learning how sound affects your internal state.

Phase 3: Integration (Sound as Regulation)
At this stage, sound becomes a tool rather than a trigger.
You intentionally use:

- Silence for grounding
- Music for emotional regulation
- Voice for self-anchoring
- Ambient sound for focus

You no longer consume sound passively. You curate it.
Your environment becomes an extension of your nervous system.

The Four Categories of Sound

Understanding sound through these four lenses helps refine your awareness:

1. Nourishing Sound

Promotes calm, clarity, or grounded energy.
Examples: soft music, nature sounds, gentle voices, intentional silence.

2. Neutral Sound

Functional background noise that does not strongly affect mood.
Examples: light household noise, white noise, ambient hums.

3. Depleting Sound

Drains energy or increases agitation over time.
Examples: aggressive media, constant commentary, chaotic audio feeds.

4. Intrusive Sound

Hijacks attention and creates stress or anxiety.
Examples: yelling, alarm-heavy content, aggressive messaging, doom-scrolling audio.

Your goal is not perfection—but awareness and choice.

The 7-Day Audio Detox Reset

This gentle reset can be done anytime you feel overstimulated.

Day 1–2: Observation

Notice what you listen to and when. No changes yet.

Day 3–4: Reduction

Reduce unnecessary sound by 30–50%. Replace with silence or breath.

Day 5: Reintroduction

Add one sound that feels regulating and supportive.

Day 6: Personalization

Choose one sound that feels like *home*—something that brings you back into your body.

Day 7: Integration

Move through the day consciously choosing sound rather than defaulting.

This is not about restriction. It is about agency.

Sound Boundaries for Daily Life

Healthy sound boundaries protect mental clarity.
Examples:

- No audio during the first 20 minutes after waking.
- Silence during emotional processing.
- Intentional music only when emotionally stable.
- No background noise during important decisions.

These are not rules. They are tools.
Boundaries create space for signal to emerge.

When Silence Feels Uncomfortable

Silence often activates unresolved material. This is not failure—it is information.

If silence feels unbearable:

- Shorten it.
- Ground your body.
- Return to sound intentionally.

You are not required to endure discomfort to heal. You are invited to approach it gradually.

Safety always comes first.

Rebuilding Trust With Your Inner Channel

As noise fades, your inner voice becomes clearer—but quieter.

It will not shout. It will suggest.

Trust builds through repetition. The more you respond to your own inner guidance, the stronger it becomes.

Over time, you will notice:

- Reduced reactivity
- Increased clarity
- Faster emotional recovery
- A sense of internal spaciousness

This is not transcendence. It is regulation.

The Long-Term Shift

An audio detox is not a one-time cleanse. It is a relationship shift.

You move from consumption to communion.

From reaction to resonance.

From noise to knowing.

Your inner world becomes a place you want to inhabit.

Closing Reflection

Sound shapes identity.

What you listen to becomes what you believe.

What you repeat becomes what you live.

By choosing your auditory environment with care, you choose your internal world with intention.

Silence is not the absence of life—it is the space where truth becomes audible.

And when you learn to listen from that place, you no longer need to escape noise.

You simply outgrow it.

Message from the Author:

I hope you enjoyed this book, I love astrology and knew there was not a book such as this out on the shelf. I love metaphysical items as well. Please check out my other books:

-Life of Government Benefits

-My life of Hell

-My life with Hydrocephalus

-Red Sky

-World Domination:Woman's rule

-World Domination:Woman's Rule 2: The War

-Life and Banishment of Apophis: book 1

-The Kidney Friendly Diet

-The Ultimate Hemp Cookbook

-Creating a Dispensary(legally)

-Cleanliness throughout life: the importance of showering from childhood to adulthood.

-Strong Roots: The Risks of Overcoddling children

-Hemp Horoscopes: Cosmic Insights and Earthly Healing

- Celestial Hemp Navigating the Zodiac: Through the Green Cosmos

-Astrological Hemp: Aligning The Stars with Earth's Ancient Herb

-The Astrological Guide to Hemp: Stars, Signs, and Sacred Leaves

-Green Growth: Innovative Marketing Strategies for your Hemp Products and Dispensary

-Cosmic Cannabis

-Astrological Munchies

-Henry The Hemp

-Zodiacal Roots: The Astrological Soul Of Hemp

- **Green Constellations: Intersection of Hemp and Zodiac**

-Hemp in The Houses: An astrological Adventure Through The Cannabis Galaxy

-Galactic Ganja Guide

Heavenly Hemp
Zodiac Leaves
Doctor Who Astrology
Cannastrology
Stellar Satvias and Cosmic Indicas
Celestial Cannabis: A Zodiac Journey
AstroHerbology: The Sky and The Soil: Volume 1
AstroHerbology:Celestial Cannabis:Volume 2
Cosmic Cannabis Cultivation
The Starry Guide to Herbal Harmony: Volume 1
The Starry Guide to Herbal Harmony: Cannabis Universe: Volume 2
Yugioh Astrology: Astrological Guide to Deck, Duels and more
Nightmare Mansion: Echoes of The Abyss
Nightmare Mansion 2: Legacy of Shadows
Nightmare Mansion 3: Shadows of the Forgotten
Nightmare Mansion 4: Echoes of the Damned
The Life and Banishment of Apophis: Book 2
Nightmare Mansion: Halls of Despair
Healing with Herb: Cannabis and Hydrocephalus
Planetary Pot: Aligning with Astrological Herbs: Volume 1
Fast Track to Freedom: 30 Days to Financial Independence Using AI, Assets, and Agile Hustles
Cosmic Hemp Pathways
How to Become Financially Free in 30 Days: 10,000 Paths to Prosperity
Zodiacal Herbage: Astrological Insights: Volume 1
Nightmare Mansion: Whispers in the Walls
The Daleks Invade Atlantis
Henry the hemp and Hydrocephalus

10X The Kidney Friendly Diet
Cannabis Universe: Adult coloring book

Hemp Astrology: The Healing Power of the Stars

Zodiacal Herbage: Astrological Insights: Cannabis Universe: Volume 2

Planetary Pot: Aligning with Astrological Herbs: Cannabis Universes: Volume 2

Doctor Who: Convergence Protocol – The Replicator War

Nightmare Mansion: Curse of the Blood Moon

The Celestial Stoner: A Guide to the Zodiac

Cosmic Pleasures: Sex Toy Astrology for Every Sign

Hydrocephalus Astrology: Navigating the Stars and Healing Waters

Lapis and the Mischievous Chocolate Bar

Celestial Positions: Sexual Astrology for Every Sign

Apophis's Shadow Work Journal: **:** A Journey of Self-Discovery and Healing

Kinky Cosmos: Sexual Kink Astrology for Every Sign

Digital Cosmos: The Astrological Digimon Compendium

Stellar Seeds: The Cosmic Guide to Growing with Astrology

Apophis's Daily Gratitude Journal

Cat Astrology: Feline Mysteries of the Cosmos

The Cosmic Kama Sutra: An Astrological Guide to Sexual Positions

Unleash Your Potential: A Guided Journal Powered by AI Insights

Whispers of the Enchanted Grove

Cosmic Pleasures: An Astrological Guide to Sexual Kinks

369, 12 Manifestation Journal

Whisper of the nocturne journal(blank journal for writing or drawing)

The Boogey Book

Locked In Reflection: A Chastity Journey Through Locktober

Generating Wealth Quickly:How to Generate $100,000 in 24 Hours

Star Magic: Harness the Power of the Universe

The Flatulence Chronicles: A Fart Journal for Self-Discovery

The Doctor and The Death Moth

Seize the Day: A Personal Seizure Tracking Journal

The Ultimate Boogeyman Safari: A Journey into the Boogie World and Beyond

Whispers of Samhain: 1,000 Spells of Love, Luck, and Lunar Magic: Samhain Spell Book

Apophis's guides:Witch's Spellbook Crafting Guide for Halloween

Frost & Flame: The Enchanted Yule Grimoire of 1000 Winter Spells

The Ultimate Boogey Goo Guide & Spooky Activities for Halloween Fun

Harmony of the Scales: A Libra's Spellcraft for Balance and Beauty

The Enchanted Advent: 36 Days of Christmas Wonders

Nightmare Mansion: The Labyrinth of Screams

Harvest of Enchantment: 1,000 Spells of Gratitude, Love, and Fortune for Thanksgiving

The Boogey Chronicles: A Journal of Nightly Encounters and Shadowy Secrets

The 12 Days of Financial Freedom: A Step-by-Step Christmas Countdown to Transform Your Finances

Sigil of the Eternal Spiral Blank Journal

A Christmas Feast: Timeless Recipes for Every Meal

Holiday Stress-Free Solutions: A Survival Guide to Thriving During the Festive Season

Yu-Gi-Oh! Holiday Gifting Mastery: The Ultimate Guide for Fans and Newcomers Alike

Holiday Harmony: A Hydrocephalus Survival Guide for the Festive Season

Celestial Craft: The Witch's Almanac for 2025 – A Cosmic Guide to Manifestations, Moons, and Mystical Events

Doctor Who: The Toymaker's Winter Wonderland

Tulsa King Unveiled: A Thrilling Guide to Stallone's Mafia Masterpiece

Pendulum Craft: A Complete Guide to Crafting and Using Personalized Divination Tools

Nightmare Mansion: Santa's Eternal Eve

Starlight Noel: A Cosmic Journey through Christmas Mysteries

The Dark Architect: Unlocking the Blueprint of Existence

Surviving the Embrace: The Ultimate Guide to Encounters with The Hugging Molly

The Enchanted Codex: Secrets of the Craft for Witches, Wiccans, and Pagans

Harvest of Gratitude: A Complete Thanksgiving Guide

Yuletide Essentials: A Complete Guide to an Authentic and Magical Christmas

Celestial Smokes: A Cosmic Guide to Cigars and Astrology

Living in Balance: A Comprehensive Survival Guide to Thriving with Diabetes Insipidus

Cosmic Symbiosis: The Venom Zodiac Chronicles

The Cursed Paw of Ambition

Cosmic Symbiosis: The Astrological Venom Journal

Celestial Wonders Unfold: A Stargazer's Guide to the Cosmos (2024-2029)

The Ultimate Black Friday Prepper's Guide: Mastering Shopping Strategies and Savings

Cosmic Sales: The Astrological Guide to Black Friday Shopping

Legends of the Corn Mother and Other Harvest Myths

Whispers of the Harvest: The Corn Mother's Journal

The Evergreen Spellbook

The Doctor Meets the Boogeyman

The White Witch of Rose Hall's SpellBook

The Gingerbread Golem's Shadow: A Study in Sweet Darkness

The Gingerbread Golem Codex: An Academic Exploration of Sweet Myths

The Gingerbread Golem Grimoire: Sweet Magicks and Spells for the Festive Witch

The Curse of the Gingerbread Golem

10-minute Christmas Crafts for kids

Christmas Crisis Solutions: The Ultimate Last-Minute Survival Guide

Gingerbread Golem Recipes: Holiday Treats with a Magical Twist

The Infinite Key: Unlocking Mystical Secrets of the Ages

Enchanted Yule: A Wiccan and Pagan Guide to a Magical and Memorable Season

Dinosaurs of Power: Unlocking Ancient Magick

Astro-Dinos: The Cosmic Guide to Prehistoric Wisdom

Gallifrey's Yule Logs: A Festive Doctor Who Cookbook

The Dino Grimoire: Secrets of Prehistoric Magick

The Gift They Never Knew They Needed

The Gingerbread Golem's Culinary Alchemy: Enchanting Recipes for a Sweetly Dark Feast

A Time Lord Christmas: Holiday Adventures with the Doctor

Krampusproofing Your Home: Defensive Strategies for Yule

Silent Frights: A Collection of Christmas Creepypastas to Chill Your Bones

Santa Raptor's Jolly Carnage: A Dino-Claus Christmas Tale

Prehistoric Palettes: A Dino Wicca Coloring Journey

The Christmas Wishkeeper Chronicles

The Starlight Sleigh: A Holiday Journey

Elf Secrets: The True Magic of the North Pole

Candy Cane Conjurations

Cooking with Kids: Recipes Under 20 Minutes

Doctor Who: The TARDIS Confiscation

The Anxiety First Aid Kit: Quick Tools to Calm Your Mind

Frosty Whispers: A Winter's Tale

The Infinite Key: Unlocking the Secrets to Prosperity, Resilience, and Purpose

The Grasping Void: Why You'll Regret This Purchase

Astrology for Busy Bees: Star Signs Simplified

The Instant Focus Formula: Cut Through the Noise

The Secret Language of Colors: Unlocking the Emotional Codes

Sacred Fossil Chronicles: Blank Journal

The Christmas Cottage Miracle

Feeding Frenzy: Graboid-Inspired Recipes

Manifest in Minutes: The Quick Law of Attraction Guide

The Symbiote Chronicles: Doctor Who's Venomous Journey

Think Tiny, Grow Big: The Minimalist Mindset

The Energy Key: Unlocking Limitless Motivation

New Year, New Magic: Manifesting Your Best Year Yet

Unstoppable You: Mastering Confidence in Minutes

Infinite Energy: The Secret to Never Feeling Drained

Lightning Focus: Mastering the Art of Productivity in a Distracted World

Saturnalia Manifestation Magick: A Guide to Unlocking Abundance During the Solstice

Graboids and Garland: The Ultimate Tremors-Themed Christmas Guide

12 Nights of Holiday Magic

The Power of Pause: 60-Second Mindfulness Practices

The Quick Reset: How to Reclaim Your Life After Burnout

The Shadow Eater: A Tale of Despair and Survival

The Micro-Mastery Method: Transform Your Skills in Just Minutes a Day

Reclaiming Time: How to Live More by Doing Less

Chronovore: The Eternal Nexus

The Mind Reset: Unlocking Your Inner Peace in a Chaotic World
Confidence Code: Building Unshakable Self-Belief
Baby the Vampire Terrier
Baby the Vampire Terrier's Christmas Adventure
Celestial Streams: The Content Creator's Astrology Manual
The Wealth Whisperer: Unlocking Abundance with Everyday Actions
The Energy Equation: Maximize Your Output Without Burning Out
The Happiness Algorithm: Science-Backed Steps to Joyful Living
Stress-Free Success: Achieving Goals Without Anxiety
Mindful Wealth: The New Blueprint for Financial Freedom
The Festive Flavors of New Year: A Culinary Celebration
The Master's Gambit: Keys of Eternal Power
Shadowed Secrets: Groundhog Day Mysteries
Beneath the Burrow: Lessons from the Groundhog
Spring's Whispers: The Groundhog's Prediction
The Limitless Mindset: Unlock Your Untapped Potential
The Focus Funnel: How to Cut Through Chaos and Get Results
Bold Moves: Building Courage to Live on Your Terms
The Daily Shift: Simple Practices for Lasting Transformation
The Quarter-Life Reset: Thriving in Your 20s and 30s
The Art of Shadowplay: Building Your Own Personal Myth
The Eternal Loop: Finding Purpose in Repetition
Burrowing Wisdom: Life Lessons from the Groundhog
Shadow Work: A Groundhog Day Perspective
Love in Bloom: 5-Minute Romantic Gestures
The Shadowspell Codex: Secrets of Forbidden Magick
The Burnout Cure: Finding Balance in a Busy World
The Groundhog Prophecy: Unlocking Seasonal Secrets
Nog Tales: The Spirited History of Eggnog
Six More Weeks: Embracing Seasonal Transitions
The Lumivian Chronicles: Fragments of the Fifth Dimension

Money on Your Mind: A Beginner's Guide to Wealth
The Focus Fix: Breaking Through Distraction
January's Spirit Keepers: Mystical Protectors of the Cold
Creativity Unchained: Unlocking Your Wildest Ideas in 2025
Manifestation Mastery: 365 Days to Rewrite Your Reality
The Groundhog's Mirror: Reflecting on Change
The Weeping Angels' Christmas Curse
Burrowed in Time: A Groundhog Day Journey
Heartbeats: Poems to Share with Your Valentine
Dino Wicca: The Sacred Grimoire of Prehistoric Magick
Courage of the Pride: Finding Your Inner Roar
The Lion's Leap: Bold Moves for Big Results
Healthy Hustle: Achieving Without Overworking
Practical Manifesting: Turning Dreams into Reality in 2025
Jurassic Pharaohs: Unlocking the Magick of Ancient Egypt and Dino Wicca
The Happiness Equation: Small Changes for Big Joy
The Confidence Compass: Finding Your Inner Strength
Whispers in the Hollow: Tales of the Forgotten Beasts
Echoes from the Hollow: The Return of Forgotten Beasts
The Hollow Ascendant: The Rise of the Forgotten Beasts
The Relationship Reset: Building Better Connections
Mastering the Morning: How to Win the Day Before 8 AM
The Shadow's Dance: Groundhog Day Symbolism
Cupid's Kitchen: Quick Valentine's Day Recipes
Valentine's Day on a Budget: Love Without Breaking the Bank
Astrocraft: Aligning the Stars in the World of Minecraft
Forecasting Life: Groundhog Day Reflections
Bleeding Hearts: Twisted Tales of Valentine's Terror
Herbal Smoke Revolution: The Ultimate Guide to Nature's Cigarette Alternative
Winter's Wrath: The Complete Survival Blueprint for Extreme Freezes.

The Groundhog's Shadow: A Tale of Seasons
Burrowed Insights: Wisdom from the Groundhog
Sensual Strings: The Art of Erotic Bondage
Whispered Flames: Unlocking the Power of Fire Play
Forgotten Shadows: A Guide to Cryptids Lost to Time
Six Weeks of Secrets: Groundhog Day's Hidden Messages
Shadows and Cycles: Groundhog Day Reflections
The Art of Love Letters: Crafting the Perfect Message
Romantic Getaways at Home: Turning Your Space into Paradise
Purrfect Brews: A Cat Lover's Guide to Coffee and Companionship
The Groundhog's Wisdom: Timeless Lessons for Modern Life
The Shadow Oracle: Groundhog Day as a Predictor
Emerging from the Burrow: A Journey of Renewal
The Language of Love: Learning Your Partner's Love Style
Authorpreneur: The Ultimate Blueprint for Writing, Publishing, and Thriving as an Author
Weathering the Seasons: Groundhog Day Perspectives
Valentine's Day Magic: A Guide to Romantic Rituals
The Shadow Chronicles: Stories of Groundhog Day
Love and Laughter: Fun Games for Valentine's Day
AstroRealty: Unlocking the Stars for Property Success
The Groundhog's Path: A Guide to Seasonal Balance
Groundhog Day Diaries: Reflections in the Shadow
The Groundhog's Light: Illuminating the Path Ahead
Valentine's Traditions from Around the World
AI Wealth Revolution: Unlocking the Trillionaire Mindset
Love Rekindled: Reigniting Passion in Relationships
Single and Thriving: Self-Love on Valentine's Day
Emerald Legends: Mystical Tales of Ireland
Green Alchemy: Harnessing Nature's Magic
The Hearts of Horror: A Valentine's Day Nightmare

The Leprechaun's Guide to Wealth and Wisdom
Dancing with the Sidhe: Celebrating the Otherworld
Shamrocks and Shadows: Mysteries of the Green Isle
Emerald Energy: Harnessing Luck and Growth
The Gingerbread Golem's Valentine: A Sweetheart's Guide to Love and Enchantment
The Celtic Knot: Weaving Life and Destiny
Green Fire: Elemental Magic for St. Patrick's Day
Clover Chronicles: Finding Your Inner Luck
Ireland's Mystical Creatures: A Field Guide
Gingerbread Golem's Love Almanac
Prowl and Thrive: The Lion's Guide to Success
Love Alchemy: Transforming Your Life Through Heart Energy
WORLD DOMINATION: Woman's Rule 3:The New Life
The Midnight Rose: A Guide to Lunar Love Spells
The Forbidden Letters: Writing Your Own Love Prophecy
Luck and Lore: St. Patrick's Day for Modern Mystics
The Green Path: A Pagan Celebration of Renewal
The Dark Architect's Guide to Reprogramming Reality
Prankster's Paradise: A Guide to Harmless Hijinks
Manifest Your Reality: The Law of Attraction Simplified
The TARDIS Owner's Manual: Understanding the Doctor's Ship: *A complete guide to the TARDIS, its technology, secrets, and mysteries*
Starlit Romance: Astrology Secrets for Finding True Love
The Time Lord's Atlas: A Complete Guide to the Whoniverse: ***A breakdown of the locations, planets, and dimensions explored in Doctor Who***
Sweetheart Shadows: The Dark Side of Love and Attraction
February Fire: Reigniting Passion in Every Area of Life
The Self-Love Toolkit: 5 Ways to Embrace Who You Are
February Sparks: Ignite Your Dreams in 28 Days

March to Success: A 31-Day Action Blueprint
Ancient Paths: The 13 Sacred Principles of Dino Wicca
Echoes of Tomorrow: Navigating the AI Revolution
The Wellness Blueprint: Balancing Mind, Body, and Soul
Green Horizons: Sustainable Living for a Better Tomorrow
The AI Wealth Code: How to Make Millions with Automation
AI-Powered Creativity: Writing, Art, and Music for Profit
Extinction Rites: Rebirthing Your Soul Through Prehistoric Magick
Sacred Serpents tarot
Celestial Enchantment blank journal
Star Strains
Culinary Journeys: Exploring Global Flavors at Home
The Hollowvale Curse
The Hollowvale Harvest
The Egg of Transformation: Awakening Your Inner Power
Blooming Into Power: A Wiccan Guide to Spring Awakening
The Nightmare Nexus: The Third Doctor's Perilous Haunting
Digital Detox: Reclaiming Your Life in a Connected World
Ostara's Path: Walking the Spiral of Renewal
The Sacred Hare
Financial Freedom: Building Wealth in the Modern Age
Spring's Cauldron: Stirring the Waters of Change
The Hollowvale Pact
Quantum Consciousness: The Science of Reality Shifting
The Hollowvale Hunger
The Sacred Waters Within: A Witch's Guide to Hydrocephalus Magick
The Raven's Nest: Building a Life of Unshakable Stability
AI and the Human Mind: The Future of Intelligence
The Hollowvale Reckoning
Timeless Love: Building and Maintaining Lasting Relationships

The Raven's Roar: Unlocking Unstoppable Confidence
Raven Sight: Awakening Intuition and Inner Wisdom
The Butterfly Effect: Small Changes, Big Transformations
Taming the Boogeyman: How to Conquer Your Inner Fears
The Magick of Green: Awakening Earth's Energy in You
The Entrepreneurial Mindset: Secrets to Business Success
The Hollowvale End
The Shadow Luck Ritual: Reclaiming Power from Your Dark Side
Spring Magick for Beginners: A Simple Guide to Seasonal Energy Work
Doctor Who: The Hollowvale Conundrum
The March of Miracles: Unlocking Synchronicities in Spring
Unveiling the Cosmos: A Guide to Stargazing and Space Exploration
The Ultimate Guide to Surviving an Economic Collapse
The AI Gold Rush: How to Profit from the AI Revolution
Bastet's Shadow: The Hidden Power of Feline Magick
The Bastet Codex: Unlocking the Goddess's Magickal Secrets
Purring Spells: Harnessing Bastet's Healing Frequencies
Bastet's Nine Lives: Rebirth, Transformation, and Immortality Spells
Primal Currents: Hydrocephalus Magick in the Path of Dino Wicca
The Digital Gold Rush: Mastering E-Commerce and Online Sales
Future Shock: Adapting to the Next Decade of Change
The Quantum Mindset: Think Like a Billionaire
Sacred Motherhood: Awakening the Divine Feminine Within
The Mother's Spellbook: Enchantments for Love, Protection, and Prosperity
The Witch's Guide to Parenting: Raising Empowered and Intuitive Children

The Magick of Motherhood: Reclaiming Your Power Through Rituals
The Pagan Path to Self-Love: A Goddess's Guide to Worth and Confidence
Wild Woman Magick: Unleashing Your Primal Power
The Money Magnet Blueprint: Unlocking Unlimited Wealth
Biohacking 101: Unlock Your Body's Full Potential
The Wild Father: A Pagan Guide to Strength and Wisdom
The Sacred Masculine: Unlocking Your Inner Power
The Druid's Compass
The Warrior's Mindset
The Father's Fire
Odin's Path
Ancestral Bonds
The House That Whispers
The Magician's Code
The Wild Hunt
The Green Man's Path
The Altar of Success
The Shadow and the Sword
The High Priestess's Guide to Energy Healing
The Lunar Mother
The Sacred Self-Care Grimoire
The Womb Wisdom Codex
The Wheel of the Mother
The Witch's Guide to Manifestation
The Q2 Reset
The Ultimate Guide to AI-Powered Passive Income
Escape the 9-5
AI Feline Fortunes
The Tear-Stained Grimoire
Razorblade Runes
Cemetery Sirens

The Midnight Wristwatch
The Town That Forgets
AI Horror & Creepypasta
The Hollow Frequency
The Breach Echo
The Quiet Between Worlds
The Sigil of Tharan-Khul
Summon the Vault of Y'ha'ten
The Becoming Codex
The Profit of Az'ra-nar
The Drowned Logos
Echoes of the Eldritch Will
The Deep Ledger
Necronomicon of Networth
Covenant of the Wealthwyrm
The Whisperer's Manifesto
The Rites of Azh-K'luth
The Ark of the Crawling Coin
The Tithe of Shadows
Inkheart Abyss
The Timewinds of Y'ha-nthlei
The Spiral Labyrinth of Azag-Nirrh
The Gallifreyan Heresy of the Black Pharaoh
The Psalms of Nyog-Sotha
Black Rain Alchemy
The Infinite Maw
The Entropic Blueprint
The Oracle of Sh'guul
The Book of Breach
The Drowned Saint's Testament
Dreamcraft of the Sleeper God
The Silence Market
Cthonomics: The Dark Wealth Algorithm

Invocation of the Ten-Eyed King
Wealthbound to the Wyrm Below
Become the Unnameable
Codex of the Sovereign Flame
Rituals of Relentless Becoming
The Shadow Ascends
The Eyes Beneath You
The Will That Wakes Worlds
Silence Is a Weapon
The Mirror That Screams
The Whisper Between Moments
The Mind That Devours Fear
The Myth of the Finished Self
The Architect of Your Madness
The Voice You've Buried
The Discipline of Madness
Stormborn: Awakening Your Inner Tempest
The Mind That Ate Time
Unbind Your Becoming
The Pact You Owe Yourself
The Devourer's Diet
The Acid That Carves the Path
The Tower You Must Burn
The Breath Between Worlds
Speak Like the Deep
The Labyrinth Within
The Spine of the Sea God
Rejection Is a Portal
The Crown You Refused
The Scar Is the Spell
The Lightless Flame
The Habit of Becoming Horrific
ChickenJockey Chaos

The Gatekeeper Within
You Are Not Your Name
The Compass of the Mad
The Archive of Unsent Letters
What the Mirror Can't Show You
The Knife You Needed
Worship Nothing, Become Everything
The Other Voice
The Body the World Forgot
The Vein of the Void
The Black Bone Codex
The Puzzle of the Hidden Self (Millennium Puzzle)
The Eye That Sees the Lie *(Millennium Eye)*
The Ring of Return (Millennium Ring)
The Rod of Relentless Will ***(Millennium Rod)***
The Tally of the Soul (Millennium Tauk/Necklace)
The Key to the Locked Timeline (Millennium Key)
The Scale of Sacred Decisions (Millennium Scales)
Inferno Bites: The UnOfficial Minecraft Lava Cookbook
Rot in the Attic
Prana: The Hidden Force of Your Infinite Self
The Shadow Realm Within: Transforming Darkness Into Destiny
The Borderland Collapse
Claws of Protection: Bastet's Defensive Magick
Mr. Ring-a-Ding's Madness
Yugioh Astrology: Celestial Deckcraft and Duel Destiny (2026–2027 Edition)
The Seal You Signed: Unlocking the Power You Once Feared
The Puzzle of Infinite Minds: Unlocking the Mentalism Hidden Within
The Eye That Mirrors the All: Secrets of Inner Reflection
Doctor Who: The Toymaker's Broadcast

Rootwake: The Carbon Covenant
Skitter Logic: Unlearning the Fear That Built You
Doctor Who: The World That Froths
Rootwake: The Fizz That Rewrites Flesh
Rootwake: Frothfather of the World
The Holly Pact: Blood Beneath the Mistletoe
The 2nd Mass Principle: Building Unbreakable Tribes
Web of Wits: A Survival Guide to Encounters with Anasi the Spider (Aunt Nancy)
The Hexbreaking Handbook: Effective Spells to Remove Curses
Pop Alchemy: Transform Your Life One Sip at a Time
The Mason Code: Leading in Unleadable Times
Petosiris and the Fifth Chamber of Thoth
The Ether Seed Within
The Parent of Tomorrow
Petosiris's Pyramid of Perpetual Wealth
Unlearn the World
Grimoire of the Hollow Tongue
Zodiac Weeds: Finding Your Strain Through the Stars
Aquarius Rises in the Bank
The Sugar God's Smile
The Skinclock Reversal: Biohacking the Face of Time
Debtburn: How to Obliterate What You Owe Forever
The Ice Cream Oracle: What Your Cone Says About Your Future
Silence Is Sovereignty: The Power of Being Unreadable
The Wind That Whispers Through Stone
Path of the Four Directions
Doctor Who: The Maestro's Symphony of Endings
Oxygen Grail: Breathing to Undo the Clock
Zodiacal Collapse: When Stars Devour Time
Teachings from the Red Sand Silence

Doctor Who: Omega – The Broken Equation
Memory Wipe Your Past: Start Over Like a MiB
Mitochondria Prime: Ignite the Core of Youth
A Nest of Roaches
Grub from the Galaxy: MiB Recipes You'll Never Forget
Whiskers of Power: Bastet's Guide to Inner Sovereignty
The Gift Must Cost Them: Negotiation Through Unequal Exchange
The Worm Guys' Wealth Code: Hustle Like an Alien
Bug Out: The Edgar Method for Ruthless Goal Setting
Weaving Life with Spiderwoman's Pattern
Doctor Who: The Rani's Renaissance
How to Get a Job (If You're a Puppygirl)
Speak Through Others: The Art of Proxy Power
T-Rex Your Trauma: Reclaim the Power of Your Primal Self
The Black Briefcase: How MiB Stay Wealthy in Silence
The Thirst Beyond Reason: Understanding Diabetes Insipidus From the Inside Out
Backwoods Witchcraft for Billionaires: The Pagan Path from Dirt Roads to Gold Roads
The Moonshine Grimoire: Fermented Spells for Abundance
The Nameless Geometry
The Wraith's Mixtape: Spellcasting with Songs of Sorrow
The Gallifreyan Gentleman: Silent Wealth, Sonic Confidence, and the Doctor's Code of Living
Sugar Water Confidence
Dino Totems: Spirit Guides from Earth's First Gods
Pumpkin Sigils & Ritual Smoke
The Hózhó Compass
The Distortus Discipline – Order from Inner Mutation
Witchcraft for the Cold-Blooded Soul
Moonlight Over the Blessingway
Water, Interrupted: When the Body Forgets How to Hold On

Deformed but Divine: Embracing Your Asymmetry
Hexes in the Henhouse: The Farm Witch's Guide to Power
The Reversed Flame: A Grimoire of Inverted Power
Salt, Cells, and Sanity: Reclaiming Balance with Diabetes Insipidus
King of the Broken: Crowning the Flawed Self
Moonlight Scars: Emo Moon Magick and the Art of Lunar Sorrow
Noose Spells: Magick of the Hanging Rope
The Goth Cathedral: Rituals of the Broken and Beautiful
The Cretaceous Codex: Dino Spirits and Fossil Magick
The Turkey Bones Ritual
Nine Lives of Manifestation: Unlocking Bastet's Reality Codes
Chaos Muscles: Building Strength from Twisted Pain
Emo Blood Magick: The Veins of Power
The 3AM Flood: Nighttime Urination, Sleep Loss, and the DI Spiral
The Silence Between the Stars
The Lemon Method: Sour Your Way to Success
Starlit Sovereign
The Rite of Twelve Gates: Walking the Gates of the Duat.
Cornbread and Conjure: Recipes for Riches and Rootwork
The Black Rose Rituals: Emo Love Spells and Obsession Magick
The Eternal Goodbye: Death Magick and Rebirth Rituals
Sinkrot: The Drain That Remembers
The Hybrid Mindset: Thinking Beyond Evolution
Bone Dry: Navigating Dehydration Before It Breaks You
Wreathcraft: Winter Sigils and Yuletide Spells
The Rite of Twelve Mouths
S'mores of the Damned: Haunted Recipes for Halloween Night

Rethink the Drink: A Beverage Survival Guide for DI Warriors
The Shadow Chord: Guitar Magick and Sonic
Malformed Yet Majestic: Leading When You Feel Wrong Inside
The Cursed Diary: Ink-Stained Spells of the Emo Soul
Anxiety Off Switch: Emergency Reset for a Fried Nervous System
The Energy Heist: How to Take Back Your Life from Drainers
Beyond the Bathroom: Rebuilding Your Social Life With DI
Coyote's Gift for Decision Makers
Ghoul-Goo: Spooky S'mores You'll Die For
Echoes in the Mirror: Scrying and Self-Destruction Magick
Thread and Thorn: Stitching Spells from Rural Cloth
The Mogwai Mind: Building Untouchable Wealth from Small Ideas
Be Your Own Guide: Trust Your Inner Compass
Hormones in Chaos: The Endocrine Puzzle of Diabetes Insipidus
ChronoCleanse: Detox Your Biological Timeline
The Limb You Hide Is the One That Saves You
Leaves, Bones, and Whisper Spells
The Dinosaur Mindset: Prehistoric Tactics for Modern Wealth
Clawing Back Control: A Bastet Method for Boundaries and Empowerment
Samhain Codes of the Forgotten
Orange Alchemy: The Autumnal Spellbook
Monster Within, Master Without
The Sigil That Sleeps
Hearthcraft: Yule Hearth Sigils and Winter Warmth Spells
Temple of the Purring Moon: Rituals from Bastet's Lineage
When the Earth Remembers Your Footsteps

Food for Mood: Eat to Heal Depression, Not Just Survive It
Witch of the Kudzu Vine: Southern Pagan Wealth Secrets
The Invisible Diagnosis: Advocating for Yourself With DI
The Coffin's Lullaby: Sleep Magick and Nightmares as Portals
Ashes of the Will: Rituals for Erasing the Self
The Fracture Rite: Shattering the Magickal Core
Funeral Candles: The Art of Emo Flame Magick
The Black Grimoire: A Blank Ritual for Writing in Absence
Phantom Thirst: A Halloween Survival Guide for Diabetes Insipidus
The Hollow Crown: Emo Royalty and Magick of the Outcast King
Sandpainting for the Soul
Falling Into Balance: Using the Extra Hour to Recalibrate Life
100 Southern Superstitions That Still Work
The DI Child: A Parent's Guide to Raising Hydrated, Happy Kids
The Jungle of Shame: Escaping the Hidden Lab of Doubt
The Witch's Toast: S'mores Spells and Creepy Confections
The Hoodoo Pantry: Spells from the Mason Jar
The Immortal Fortune: Secret Wealth Lessons from Captain Jack Harkness
The Specter's Embrace: Magick for Channeling Ghostly Lovers
Grateful Waters: A Thanksgiving Survival Guide for Diabetes Insipidus
The Seizure Gospel
Harvestbind: Autumn Sigils and Samhain Spells
Doctor Who: The Algorithmic Awakening
Silent Nights, Steady Waters: A Christmas Survival Guide for Diabetes Insipidus
The Extra Hour Effect: How One Hour Can Transform Everything

Blade Between the Breaths

Running with the Mountain Shadows

Echoes of the Failed Experiment – Becoming a Living Legacy

Swamp Witches & River Ghosts: Real Southern Hauntings

Cornbread Prophecies: Magical Recipes from a Southern Table

Doctor Who: The Signal in the Star

Bloomcraft: Spring Sigils and Equinox Enchantments

Vanisher: How to Disappear from the Internet Without Losing Your Life

The Ultimate Christmas Cookie Cookbook

The Unbreakable Parent: How to Mentally Survive Raising Kids in a Broken World

Time Debt: How to Reclaim the Hours You Didn't Know You Lost

One Month, One Million: Unconventional Cash Creation Tactics

Doctor Who: The Cyber Conversion Protocol

Black Friday Frenzy: The Art of Finding Hidden Online Deals

The Grimoire Buried Under the Apple Tree

Digital Couponing Masterclass: Your Step-by-Step Guide to Black Friday Savings

The Fire Inside the Flint

Shadows on the Ceiling: The Emo Guide to Astral Magick

The Bone-Eaters Beneath Us

Black Friday Bundle Blueprint: Creating Irresistible Product Packages for Maximum Sales

Thirteen Nights of Unbinding

Doctor Who: Engines of Influence

Pumpkin Spice Alchemy: Recipes of Fire and Frost

When Raptor Met Rexy: Prehistoric Lessons in Wild Romance

Oblivion's Candle: Burn the Path Behind You

Campfire Curses and Chocolate: A Halloween S'mores Grimoire
The Wallet That Wasn't Mine: Breaking Free from Inherited Scarcity
The Cola Zodiac: What Your Fizz Says About Your Fate
Frostfire Fortune: Unlocking Winter's Hidden Prosperity
Signal Jamming: Detox Your Brain from Info Overload
The Dust of the Forgotten Rite
The Golden Cat Sigils: Drawing Power in Bastet's Name
Mud Magick: The Prosperity of Getting Dirty
Savory Spicefall: Beyond the Pumpkin Pie
Pumpkin Spice Apothecary Kitchen
The Pumpkin Spice Economy: Turning Trends into Billions
The Ember Veil: 13 Nights of Fire Magick
Financial Freeze: When Earning Triggers Panic
The Gingerbread Alchemist: Sweet Recipes with a Twist
Biosynth Power: Programming Yourself from Scratch
Echoes from the Talking Circle
Truffle Alchemy: Fungus of Fortune
Spores of Power: The Truffle Witch's Handbook
Doctor Who: The Tower That Speaks
The Mycelium Veil: Truffle Magick Unbound
Broke But Ashamed: Healing the Shame Wound of Debt
The Evergreen Mind: Growth Through Winter Stillness
The Black Veil Truffle Rite
The Voice Beneath Symbols
Witchlight on the Bayou: Swamp Spells for Sovereignty
I Grew Up Poor and Now I Sabotage My Success
The Lantern of Hollow Souls
Shutdown Survival: A Citizen's Guide to Thriving When Government Stops
When Abundance Feels Like a Threat: Healing the Hidden Fears of Enough

The Scarecrow Grimoire
Owls of the October Veil
Candlewax and Curses: A Halloween Spellbook
Excavating the Inner Fossil – Transforming Fossilized Thoughtforms into Tools of Power
The Yule Witch's Spellbook: Magick for the Holiday Season
Haunted Christmas: Ghost Stories for Winter Nights
The Christmas Survival Guide: Thriving Through the Chaos
The Bone Orchard Rites
Haunted Commerce: The Ghost in the Marketplace
When Money Triggers the Inner Child
Silent Night with the Silence: A Christmas Thriller
The Lightning Crown: Living and Leading Through Seizures
TARDIS Tidings: Festive Stories from the Whoniverse
Autumn Reset: Slowing Down Without Falling Behind
The Trillion Dollar Soul: Rewriting the Currency of Reality
Truffle Eclipse Magick
Micro-Manifestations: Quick Magick That Works
5-Minute Rituals for Busy Witches
The Marshmallow Massacre: Halloween Treats with a Sinister Twist
Blood and Blackberry Thorns
Magickal Mornings: Rituals for a Blessed Christmas Day
Embers of the All-Hallows Fire
The Pumpkin Market Collapse
The Hour You Gained: Transforming Time Into Power
The Chamber Must Be Sealed: Mastering the Power of Controlled Access
The Cursed Manuscript of Petosiris
The Festive Hearth: Creating Holiday Traditions
Darkness Rising: Thriving as Nights Grow Longer
Harvesting Time: Turning the Year's End Into Your New Beginning

Petosiris and the 13th Zodiac Key

Wagewound: When Paychecks Become Identity Prisons

Walls That Watch

The Silent Feast: Rituals of Power in the Longest Night

The Distortus Legacy : Becoming a Deformed King in a Perfect World

The Hollow Masks

The Gratitude Furnace: Forging Gold from Thanks

Feast of Inner Gold: Eating for Energy and Enlightenment

Haunted Commerce: The Season of Spending Spirits

Fear Bonds: How Panic Creates Profit

Black Friday E-Commerce Playbook: Sales Tactics to Skyrocket Your Holiday Revenue

Budgeting for Black Friday: A Holiday Savings Planner

Haunting the Harvest Moon

The Warrior's Water: Emergency Preparedness for People With DI

The First Sip of the Year: A New Year's Survival Guide for Diabetes Insipidus

Doctor Who: The Thirteenth Node

The Unseen Struggle: Mental Health, Anxiety, and Chronic Thirst

The Hearth's Hidden Ledger: Counting Energies as Currency

The Gift Alchemist: Turning Any Offering Into Gold

The Papyrus of the Bound Spirit

The Magick of Leftovers: Transmutation in the Fridge

Frost and Fortune: Christmas Wealthcraft for the Modern Magus

Last-Minute Gifts: Creative Ideas on a Budget

10 Secrets to Surviving Holiday Crowds

The Witch's Dow Jones

The Witches' Graveyard Shift

Pumpkin Sigils: Carving Rites for Midnight Power

The Secret Shopper's Black Friday Guide: How to Get Early Access and VIP Deals
Fever in the Foundation
The Neuralyzer Reset: Reprogram Your Morning Routine
Lightning Lessons of the White Painted Woman
The Enchanted Snowflake
The Magic Sip: Surviving Disney Parks with Diabetes Insipidus
The One Who Draws Through You
Santa's Secrets: A Magical Holiday Planner
Silent Bells, Loud Miracles: Self-Help for the Season of Stillness
The Sugar Spell Codex: Confectionary Magick of Christmas
Autumn Hexcraft: Fallen Leaves, Fallen Barriers
Sleep Like a Fortress: Build a Life Where Insomnia Can't Survive
Nowhere Was Ever Home
Christmas Under the Stars: A Celestial Holiday Guide
Rentproof: How to Never Be Evicted Again
Workless: Escape the 9-5 Without Being Broke
The Gilded Gift: A Wealth Altar for Christmas Morning
The Black Friday Grimoire
The Hollowing: Ceremonies of Spiritual Collapse
Doctor Who: The Nameless Signal
Where the Eagle Hides His Courage
The Dwarf Tyrant's Ascent: Claiming Power in a World of Giants
The Currency of the Dead: Trading with Spectral Bankers
The Icebound Witch: Survival and Magick in the Cold
The Emergency Money Mind: Constant Crisis, Zero Calm
Thirst & Roses: A Valentine's Survival Guide for Diabetes Insipidus

Springing Into Clarity: Mastering the Energy Shift of Daylight Saving

Speed of the Nanotyrant: Agile Strategies for Life's Hunt

The 90-Day Reset: A Science-Backed Guide to Reinvent Yourself Before the New Year

The Coil of Thorns

Timegates Unleashed

Dopamine Fasting 2.0: Rewiring Your Brain in a World of Overstimulation

The Nanotyrannus Mutation: Embracing Your Differentiated Form

Unwritten January: How to Use the Blank Page of the Year to Re-Author Your Life

Feast of the Forgotten Spirits: Ancestor Magick for the Holidays

The Burnout Codex: A System for Thriving Beyond Stress

I Don't Deserve to Have Money

When the King Doesn't See You: The Shadow Predator's Guide

The Reset Ritual :A Guide to Shedding Last Year's Weight—Emotional and Physical—by Spring Cleaning Your Soul

Calendar Alchemy: Learn to Bend Time and Productivity around Your Natural Rhythms

The Mirror Contract: A One-Sentence Agreement with Yourself that Unlocks Real Change

The Nile Formula: Sacred Flow for Millionaire Minds

Forward Momentum: Productivity Rituals for the Lost Hour

Harvest Gold: Wealth Magick of Pumpkin Spice Commerce

The Magick of Christmas Lights: Illuminating Holiday Rituals

Cranberry Crown: Royal Self-Worth through Ritual Meals

Petosiris and the Worms of the Feathered Throne

The Evergreen Equation: Self-Help for Sustained Growth

The Rain Will Wash Us Away: Emo Weather Magick
Snowlight Shadows: Magick Under Frozen Stars
Doctor Who: Merger of Empires
The Light Within the Feast: Magickal Wealth of Yuletide Flame
Momentum Machines: Small Habits Designed to Snowball into Unstoppable Forward Motion
Calm Spells: Magickal Solutions for Anxiety Relief
Santa's Final List: The Naughty Never Leave
The Mystic's Guide to Banishing Worry
The Silence Dividend: Turning Quiet Mornings into Compounding Growth All Year
Charmed Stillness: Rituals to Ease the Mind
Blood Spiral Ascension
The Vanishing Heart Invocation
Crystal Calm: Harnessing Stones for Anxiety
The Nano Tyrant Code: Strength in the Small Predator
The Energy Ledger: Accounting Methods for Vitality, Not Just Money
Snowglobe Mindset: Shake Up Your Thoughts, Settle Into Peace
The Weight of the Feather: Anubis's Codes for Soul Balance
Pocket Peppermint Power: Tiny Rituals for Big Holiday Energy
Shadowkeeper of the Golden Jackal: Anubis's Path to Energetic Protection
The Witch's Breath: Anxiety Relief Through Magickal Breathing
The Tiny Ember: Pocket Motivation for Cold Days
Stocking Sorcery: Mini Spells for Holiday Luck and Prosperity
Warm Hands, Steady Heart: Micro Grounding for Winter Anxiety

The Fourteenth Doctor: A New Beginning (David Tennant, 2022–2023)

The Fifteenth Doctor: Rewriting the Stars
(Ncuti Gatwa, 2023–2025)

Santa's Shortcut to Success: Micro Habits for a Better New Year

The Midnight Cocoa Manifesto: Comfort Rituals for Hard Nights

Why I Can't Save: Trauma Blocks to Financial Planning

Dino Brain, Mega Goals: Rewire Yourself for Savage Success.

Jurassic Profit: Unearth Your Inner Millionaire Fossil

Scales & Softness: Dating with Dino Heart

Carnotaurus Dreams.

Red Willow Thinking.

Reindeer Resilience: How to Keep Going When You're Exhausted

Candlewick Courage: Lighting Strength in Dark Seasons.

Elf-Mode Focus: Fast Attention Fixes for Busy Seasons

Futureproof Feelings: Emotional Skill-Building for Resilience No Matter What the New Year Brings

The 90-Day Rewire: Transform Your Neural Pathways Before Spring Blooms

Jolly Rich: Christmas Micro-Money Magick for Fast Prosperity.

Gingerbread Gratitude: Mini Practices for a Happier Holiday

Trauma-Spending: When Money Becomes a Drug

Goal Skeletons: Build Minimalist Frameworks for Resolutions That Last

The Snarl Strategy: Growling Back at a World That Silenced You

The Hourglass Reset: Reclaiming What the Clock Took

Yule Claw: Dino Rites of Light in the Darkness

Sacred Circles: Grounding Rituals for Anxious Souls

Clockstopper's Gut: Rebuilding the Core of Time

Winterfire Drive: Harness the Cold Season's Stillness to Ignite Deep Motivation

The 5-Minute Productivity Hack: Small Steps to Big Results

Light Ascending: A Self-Help Guide to Longer Days

Inner Economy: Trade Self-Doubt for Confidence Like a High-Value Currency

Simple Success: Decluttering Your Life for Better Results

The Resilient Mind: Thriving in Tough Times

The 2026 Playbook: Mastering the Year Ahead

The Spring Sleep Solution: Conquering Fatigue After Time Change.

The Hormonal Compass: Navigate Back to Your Youth

Golden Vision: Eating for Your Eye Color with the Power of Ghee

Lionhearted Love: Strength in Relationships

MiB Mindset: Think Like a Cosmic Agent

The Ladder of Small Wins: Climb Out of Stagnation by Stacking Micro-Victories

The Momentum Hour: Gaining More in Less Time.

The Year of You: A Self-Help Blueprint for Unapologetic Self-Ownership

The Dust That Watches You Back.

The Astral Parent

Shadow of the King: The Nanotyrannus Parable

Tiny Tidings of Triumph: Small Wins That Change Your Life

Dwarf Tyrant Rising: When You're the One They Overlook

The Bank Account Mirror: Healing How You See Yourself Through Money

Cretaceous Black

When Love Costs Too Much: Romantic Triggers and Financial Wounds

Dream-Eater's Guide to Wealth

Unzipped Reality: The Jacket That Opens Portals

The Power of No: How to Set Boundaries and Get Rich

Keeper of the Desert Veil: Anubis's Teachings on Illusion & Truth

Redacted Stargates: Stories the SGC Buried

The Clock That Dripped Time

Doctor Who: The Silent Acquisition

Hairline Manifestation: Unlocking Power at the Edge of Thought

Cash-Eater Crickets: How Insects Predict Economic Collapse

Dead Pet Whisperer: Grief Alchemy from the Other Side

The Love Algorithm Is Broken: Hack Romance Before It Hacks You

The Rite of the 8-Limbed Seal

Melt the Moon: A Fire Ritual to Reshape Emotion

Venomous Miracles: Healing Through the Poison Path

Wealth Without Water: The Post-Aquatic Rich Life

The Butterfly Betrayal: When Change Turns on You

The Quiet Upgrade: How Humans Are Secretly Rebuilding Themselves Without Asking Permission

Nobody Taught Us This: The Missing Human Manual for Money, Energy, and Self-Respect

You Were Never Broken: Why Most People Are Reacting Normally to an Unstable World

After the Noise Ends: How Humans Reset When the World Finally Goes Quiet

The Month That Tells the Truth: Why January Reveals What the Rest of the Year Hides

Tremors Party Unleashed: The Ultimate Guide to a Graboids Birthday Bash

Cold Start Human: Rebooting Motivation Without Forcing Momentum

The Year that doesn't start until they say

Love Without Performance: What Connection Looks Like When No One Is Watching

February Is a Mirror: What Love Exposes About You

How We Learned Love Wrong: Uninstalling Cultural Myths About Connection

You Are Not Too Much: Why Needing Love Is Not a Flaw

The Crooked Fence Covenant: Backwoods Boundaries and Witch Wealth

The Day That Keeps Repeating: Why Your Life Feels Stuck—and How to Shift It Gently

Nothing Changes Until Something Softens: Escaping Repetition Without Violence to Yourself

Same Life, Different Ending: How Tiny Choices Rewrite Repetition

The Loop Isn't Punishment: Why You're Being Asked to Learn, Not Suffer

Panic at the Register: Retail Anxiety and Public Shame

The Secret Formula to Becoming an Influencer in 90 Days

The New Rich: How to Retire by 35

Digital Nomad Secrets: How to Travel the World and Make Millions

Burn Your Waiting Room: Escape the Delay Spiral

Strapped for Pleasure: A Complete Guide to Pegging and Strap-On Play

Locked in Desire: A Guide to Chastity Play and Intimate Control

Burrowing into History: Groundhog Day Through the Ages

The Shadow Forecast: The Science of Groundhog Day

Choice Cascades: How One Decision in January Sets Ripples for the Whole Year

The Anti-Anxiety Blueprint: Mastering Fear and Stress for Success

The Ancestral Path of the Jackal Priest

Get Some Tarot cards: https://www.makeplayingcards.com/sell/apophis-occult-shop

Get some shirts: https://www.bonfire.com/store/apophis-shirt-emporium/

Instagrams:
@apophis_enterprises,
@apophisbookemporium,
@apophisscardshop
Twitter: @apophisenterpr1
Tiktok:@apophisenterprise
Youtube: @sg1fan23477
Hive: @sg1fan23477
CheeLee: @SG1fan23477

Podcast: Apophis Chat Zone: https://open.spotify.com/show/5zXbrCLEV2xzCp8ybrfHsk?si=fb4d4fdbdce44dec

Newsletter: https://apophiss-newsletter-27c897.beehiiv.com/

If you want to support me or see posts of other projects that I have come over to: **buymeacoffee.com/mpetchinskg**

I post there daily several times a day

www.ingramcontent.com/pod-product-compliance
Lightning Source LLC
LaVergne TN
LVHW022008200926
848481LV00007B/2277
9798295526046